The Trouble with Patrick

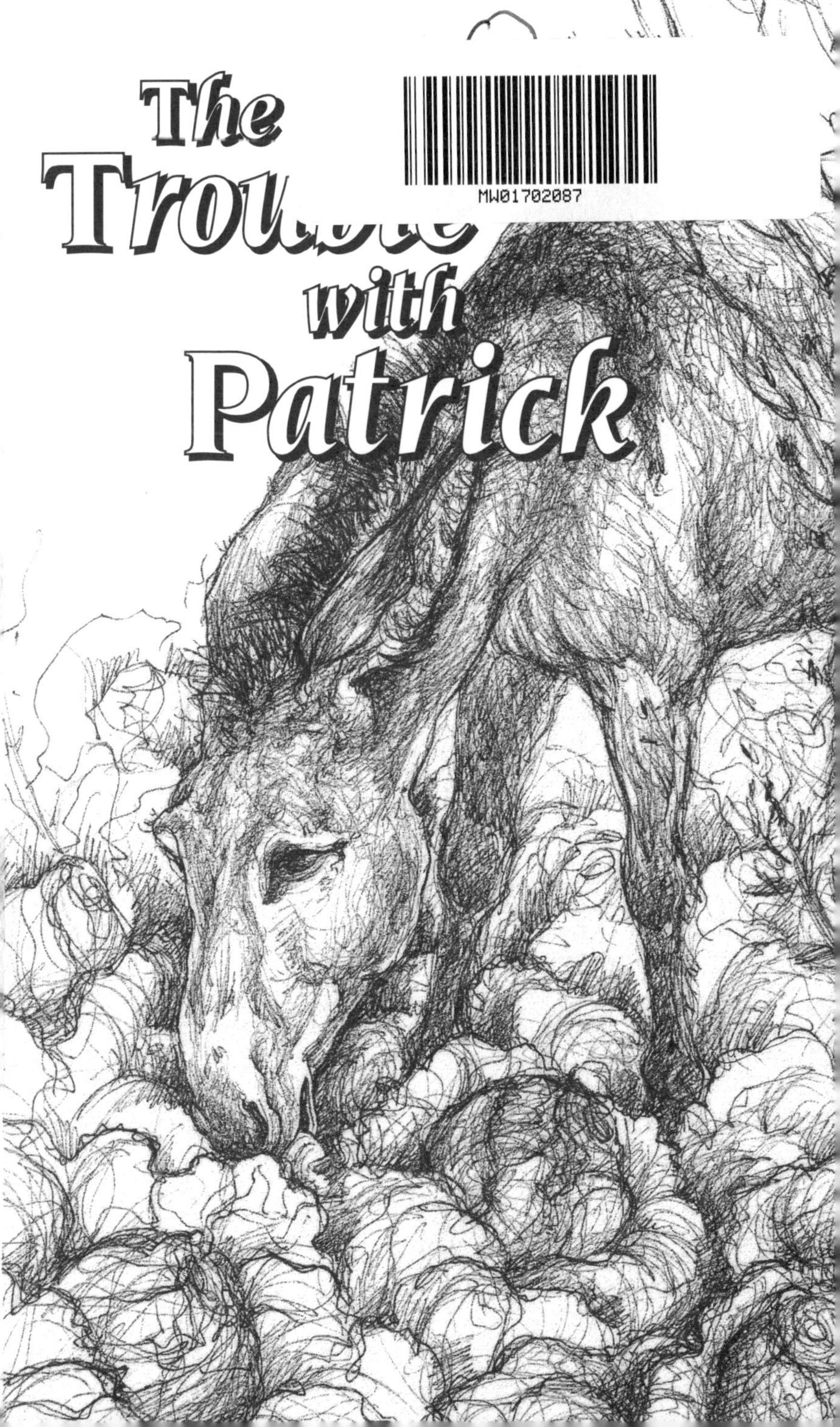

Contents

Chapter 1

Dreams and Reality

Saina leaned against the fence and looked around the fields dotted with grazing sheep.

"What this field needs is a pony," she said to herself as she imagined the sight of a pony trotting toward her.

It would nicker with affection as it nuzzled her hands for an apple, its steamy breath warming her fingers. It would stand quietly as she threw on the blanket and saddle, and lean against her as she tightened the girth. It would shake its head as she buckled the bridle and scratched between its ears. It would fidget with impatience as she swung herself onto the saddle.

They would canter around the field, cleanly clearing the poles set up for jumps.

Then they would gallop furiously toward the house, her pony's mane and tail flowing. They would slow down to a walk. She would stop; dismount; remove the saddle, blanket, and bridle; and give the pony a good grooming and a drink of water. Then, with delight, it would snort, spin, and gallop up the field, flicking its heels with the joy of being alive and belonging to her, Saina Frances Jackson!

Saina sighed and pushed herself away from the fence. The barbed wire had left purple marks on her hands. She rubbed them together and thrust them into her pockets as she walked up the path, toward home. Blackbirds fled, chattering their anger at her for disturbing their nest-building activities.

"What do you think you have to complain about, you stupid blackbirds?" Saina called resentfully. "You like it here."

"I'm sorry, Saina," her father said. "I'd love to get you a pony, but honestly, we just can't afford it at the moment. You know it took every last cent to buy this little farm. And it'll take a year or two to get us up and running before we can even think about getting a pony. Anyway, you'd need a saddle and bridle, a brush, riding gear; I bet there's lots of other things, too. A pony is just the basic expense. Look, wait until we can afford to get everything, and then you can start. Remember, Saina, we've still got a lot of work left to do on the house!"

Saina sighed. She could see her pony disappearing far into the future. The house was kind of a dump, and she knew from her father's tone during his speech that he meant what he said.

They had moved from the city to the country two weeks ago – Mom, Dad, Saina, and Pete, the baby.

"You'll love it out there," Dad had said.

But Saina hated it. From their normal home, with its red bricks and gray-tiled roof, they had moved to their new house. The wooden siding badly needed painting, and the peeling, green roof looked like a map of the world. The high ceilings inside were stained where the roof had leaked. The ceilings even sagged in places, with stray pieces of straw from birds' nests poking through. The carpet was old and covered with unidentified stains caused by years of neglect.

Old Mr. Irvine, from whom they'd bought the house, had done little over the last few years to keep it repaired. The farm was in pretty much the same condition. Saina's father had already been busy on the weekends, mending fences and cutting hedges. The only area where Mr. Irvine had made any effort was in caring for the garden around the house. A flourishing vegetable garden gave them new potatoes, broccoli, carrots, cabbage, and parsnips for their dinner. The flower garden was a mass of color, and whenever Saina's mother got depressed with the house, she would go outside and walk around, looking at the flowers. She always felt better about the place when she returned.

"This house has character," Saina's mom said, sounding cheerful. "And it's up to us to bring it out!"

But Saina thought the house was a dump. She missed her bright, cheerful bedroom in the city, with its creamy wallpaper and the warm red curtains that she'd grown up with. She also missed her friends. It was only the dream of having her own pony that had made the thought of living in the country bearable, and it didn't seem as if that dream would ever come true.

Chapter 2

The Surprise

Saina knew something was up as soon as she saw her father walk in that Friday after work. He had that small half-smile – the same half-smile she had seen on his face many times before when he wanted to tease her, hide something from her, or tell her a secret. That look had been on his face when he'd told Saina about Mom expecting Pete. It had been there again when he had told them about the farm.

"Hello, Saina. How was school?"

"Why are you looking like that?" Saina asked, instead of answering his question.

"Like what?" Dad said, and smiled.

Saina's father owned a second-hand shop in the city. He traded in old furniture and pretty much anything else that could be of use to someone. Saina's mom called it junk, but her father called it "recycled usables." He used to bring things home – like the automatic egg-sheller, which had ground up the eggs and the shell together; and the one thousand–piece jigsaw puzzle, which turned out to have 993 pieces.

Saina's mother kept telling Dad not to bring home any more junk, but every now and then he still did. Had he brought something home now? Was that why he looked so mysterious?

"What are you going to tell me, Dad?" Saina asked.

"Nothing. Why?"

"You've got that look on your face."

"What look? Have I got a look on my face, Denise?" he asked Saina's mother.

Saina looked at her. She had a strange look on her face, too. It wasn't like the "mouse-who-got-the-cheese" look that Dad had. In fact, it was the opposite – more of an "I'm-not-sure-that-I-like-this" look.

"What's going on around here? Don't tease me. Please tell me, Dad!" Saina begged her father.

"Well, I suppose I'd better confess." Dad grinned. "Go and look in the field next to the barn."

Saina looked at her dad. He was smiling. Her heart missed a beat. It couldn't be, could it?

She dropped her books on the floor and shot out the door. She flew down the path, through the back entrance, and was tearing across the lawn in an instant. It must be! Dad wouldn't look like that unless he'd got her a... She bolted up to the fence. Saina couldn't believe her eyes. Standing there, grazing noisily on clumps of grass, its ears perkily sticking straight up from its head, was a little, gray donkey!

The donkey lifted its head and brayed, "Eee-yaw! Eee-yaw!" Then it lowered its head again and continued grazing, looking up at her every once in a while, between large mouthfuls of grass.

Saina took a deep breath and then let it out slowly. Her vision blurred. She blinked hard to clear the tears as she stood there, speechless. Her mind raced with thoughts. Was this some sort of joke? What was her father thinking? Maybe she'd missed something. Her eyes swept across the field. It was empty except for the donkey.

She closed her eyes for a few moments. Maybe the donkey was an illusion, and when she opened her eyes, a pony would be there after all. But when she opened her eyes, all she saw was a short, bristle-faced donkey!

"What do you think? Isn't he cute?" her father said from behind her. Saina's mom stood beside him, with Pete in her arms.

"Is this going to be Pete's donkey?" Saina asked carefully, trying to hide the tremor in her voice. She knew she hadn't quite managed it, for she saw her mom press her dad's arm in warning.

"No, he's yours. Isn't he cute?" Dad repeated. (Perhaps he hadn't felt the warning pressure on his arm.)

"Isn't he cute? What do I think?" Saina repeated her father's words. "I'll tell you what I think. It's a stupid, little donkey! What would anyone want with a stupid, stupid donkey?" she shouted. Then she turned and ran down the path, toward the back of the farm. She ran until she was so out of breath she had to stop. She walked on slowly until she reached the gate.

"A donkey! How could anyone think I wanted a donkey when all I've ever asked for is a pony?" Saina shouted. She picked up a stick and threw it blindly, startling a grazing sheep. The sheep backed away and ran off, then it stopped and looked back at her. It cautiously resumed its grazing, looking at her now and then in case she did something unexpected.

Saina's eyes blurred again, and she gripped the gate fiercely. "I hate this place!" she cried out at the sheep. "No friends, nothing to do. What do I want more than anything? A pony. What have I got? A donkey! A scruffy, ugly, little donkey! Did I want to live here? No! Do I like this place? I hate it!"

For several minutes, Saina poured out all her pent-up frustrations. The sheep curiously looked at her for a while, and then it decided she seemed to be harmless, and it carried on eating.

Finally, Saina ran out of horrible things to say about the farm, her father, and life in general, and stopped her tirade. She felt a little better. She looked around. Only the grazing sheep had witnessed her outburst. She leaned on the gate for a few more minutes, and then slowly headed home.

Chapter 3

The Bargain

At the dinner table that night, Saina deliberately avoided looking at her parents as she ate her meal in silence.

Finally, her father spoke. "I'm sorry you don't like our new pet. Your mother said you wouldn't be impressed, but I thought that if I couldn't get you a pony, then perhaps you would like a friendly little donkey." He caught Saina's flicker of anger, and quickly continued. "I happened to be at a clearance sale today of a family that is moving overseas. I was packing up some purchases at the end of the sale, when the man who is moving asked me if I knew of anyone who was looking for a donkey. Well, I thought quickly and said, 'I know someone with a kind heart, and an empty space in her life, who may like a donkey.' I know you wanted a pony, but I thought, well, if you could look after the donkey, then it would tell me that you could look after a pony, and I could think seriously about getting one for you..." His voice trailed away.

Through Saina's gloom, a faint glimmer of hope appeared. She asked, "Do you mean that if I can show you I can do a good job taking care of this donkey, then you'll get me a pony?"

"I said I'll think seriously about it. I can't make any promises. You'll have to be patient. There are so many other things we have to do first. Like renovating the house so that you and your mom are as happy living here as I am." Dad looked at her expectantly. "Well?"

"How long will I have to wait?"

"I don't know. It depends on many things. But the most important thing is how well you look after the donkey. His name, by the way, is Patrick."

Saina thought hard. Patrick wasn't a pony, but she could practice grooming him, and maybe she could teach him a few things. It could be worth it if it meant she could get her pony sooner. And after all, she knew her dad had meant well, and she didn't want to be ungrateful. She looked across the table at her father. "OK, I'll give it a try."

"Good girl," her father said with relief. "Now, there's some gear for him in the barn. You sort it out and look after it. There's a sack of oats; you'll need to feed him every day. He also needs water and exercise each day, and I guess the rest is just generally looking after him and seeing that he gets everything he needs. He's all yours."

Dad leaned back in his chair and beamed at Saina's mother.

Chapter 4

Patrick

After dinner, Saina went out to the barn and poured some oats into a bucket. She picked up the grooming brush, and with bucket and brush in hand, walked over to the pasture. She opened the gate and walked up to the donkey, who stood quietly looking at her.

Saina dropped the brush, held out the bucket, and said, "Hello, stupid donkey, or Patrick, or whatever your name is. Let's be clear about this. I didn't ask for a donkey. I don't want you. I don't like you. And as soon as I get my pony, you'll be taking second place. Do you understand?"

The donkey quickly lowered its head and began to eat noisily. It snuffled and snorted with pleasure, and in a few minutes, it had devoured every grain. It then sniffed hopefully around the bottom of the empty bucket, looking for more.

"Don't be greedy," Saina said. She pulled the bucket away and turned to pick up the brush she'd brought out.

Suddenly, she felt her feet leave the ground as a great shove from behind left her sprawled flat on the grass.

"Hey!" Saina yelled, as she scrambled to her feet to find Patrick standing beside her, snuffling at the bucket again.

"Why, you rotten thing!" she cried, and grabbed the bucket away from him. "Just for that, you won't get the grooming I was going to give you!"

The donkey stood quietly, looking at her with big, sad eyes.

"And don't look at me like that – you started this!" She closed the gate and stalked away toward the barn.

"Eee-yaw! Eee-yaw!" called Patrick.

"And the same to you!" Saina yelled over her shoulder.

She returned the bucket and brush to the shed, and was walking toward the house, dreaming of the pony she didn't have, when she heard a loud, "Eee-yaw! Eee-yaw!" behind her. She spun around. There, trotting across the driveway, heading for the garden, was Patrick! She must have left the gate unlatched. He trotted through the back entrance and across the lawn, and began nibbling some cabbage.

"Get out of there!" Saina cried as she ran toward the donkey, who tore off a last leaf of cabbage, and chewing furiously, scampered across the garden to begin grazing on some flowers. Saina ran after him shouting loudly. Patrick ripped out a mouthful of flowers and galloped away. He headed back into the vegetable garden, where he trampled his way through the rows of carrots to begin munching on the cabbage again.

"Good-bye, pony!" thought Saina as she ran back toward Patrick. He quickly swerved away again and ran to the big willow tree that grew at the edge of the garden.

He began tugging at the leaves with his teeth. When he tried to run with a mouthful, there was a loud cracking sound and a branch from the tree broke off and fell onto him, covering him with fine branches and leaves. Clamping his mouth firmly onto his prize, Patrick bolted across the lawn, looking like a war-horse under camouflage. He sped out of the garden and over to the barn, where he stopped and began calmly grazing on the cascade of willow leaves he had carried with him.

Saina ran toward Patrick. Dragging his leafy treasure, he trotted back into the field he'd come from. Saina quickly ran to the gate and angrily slammed it shut, sliding the latch across with a thump. She leaned on the fence and watched the donkey, who was quietly grazing on the leaves, as if nothing had happened.

"There's plenty of grass in here for a day or two," Saina said sternly. "Now, you behave yourself, or I'll... I'll... sell you to someone mean!"

"Eee-yaw," Patrick called, as if he thought it was a joke.

"I mean it, Patrick!" Saina sharply replied. "You see if I don't!"

As Saina came through the door, her mom asked, "How's Patrick?" Her mouth twisted, and she seemed to be having trouble talking. Saina thought she saw tears in her mother's eyes.

"Fine, Mom," Saina replied. "Why? Are you all right?" she asked with concern.

"There seems to be some rather unusual footprints across the garden and lawn," her mom said. "And part of the tree is missing!" She suddenly doubled over, burst out laughing, and continued to laugh until tears streamed down her face. It was some time before she regained her composure. "Oh, Saina. I wish I'd had a video camera!"

"Were you looking out the window?" Saina asked. She laughed, too. "I guess it must have looked pretty funny. I think I left the gate unlatched when I was feeding him before. I've put him back now. And he didn't eat too much."

Saina's mom managed to stop laughing, and said, "Seriously though, Saina, you've got to keep an eye on him. That means making sure you've closed the gate. I did have a good laugh, but he could really make a mess of the garden, and I want those vegetables and flowers left for us!" She grinned again. "Oh, my goodness! It was one of the funniest things I've seen in a long time. It really brightened up my day. You should have seen the look on your face!"

Saina felt relieved. At least things weren't too bad. Mom may not even mention this to Dad, hopefully.

"Sorry, Mom," Saina said. "It won't happen again, I promise. You wait, Patrick," she muttered under her breath.

The first sight that greeted Saina in the morning as she pulled back the curtains was Patrick standing in the garden chewing on a mouthful of cabbage.

"Oh, no!" Saina groaned. She hastily got dressed and sneaked out the back door. "Shoo!" she hissed as she herded him out of the garden. He casually trotted across the lawn, heading back toward his field.

Saina looked at the destruction. There were only two heads of cabbage left. The rest had been neatly chewed off at the stalk. The remainder of the garden had been thoroughly trampled. It looked like a stampede had been through it. A pile of donkey droppings decorated the path.

Saina ran out after the donkey and chased him with her arms flapping wildly in the air. Just as she caught up with him, Patrick swerved toward her. Saina lost her balance and slipped, landing in a large puddle of mud.

She sat there on the path. Tears of pain and anger welled up in her eyes. That donkey was the worst! She hadn't even wanted him in the first place, and now she had to do a good job of looking after him or she'd never get her pony. She had promised to keep the gate shut, and she must have left it open again. Her mom would be mad at her, and her dad would be upset, because he'd gotten the donkey in the first place, and believed Saina when she had promised to look after it well – just as well as if it were a pony. What a mess!

"I'll get you for this, Patrick!" Saina seethed from the ground.

Painfully, she got up and went over to the field where Patrick stood sullenly, behind the open gate. She was sure she'd shut it earlier, and latched it carefully. She double-checked it this time, and tied some twine around it to make sure it would stay shut. Then she made an ugly face at Patrick as he gave her his innocent, big-eyed look. Saina turned in disgust, and slowly walked back to the house to face the music.

Chapter 5

The Find

"Oh, hi, Mom," Saina said nervously as she kicked off her boots and opened the front door.

"Hi, sweetie. What have you been doing?" her mom asked as she buttered some toast.

"Um, putting Patrick back into his field. Mom, um... I don't know how, but Patrick got into the garden again last night."

"Oh, no! Saina, I told you to be more careful with that gate!" her mom said as she dropped the toast and hurried outside to look at the damage. Saina cringed as she heard her mother's cry of anguish.

When Saina's mom returned, she angrily said, "The only good thing about this place was the garden, and now it's a wreck!

How could you be so careless?" This time, the tears in her eyes weren't from laughter.

"I don't know how it happened!" Saina cried. "I'm sure I closed the gate securely. I'm sure I did!"

"Well, you couldn't have! Saina, I'm very disappointed in you. You wanted a pony to look after, and you can't remember to close a gate properly. Look at my beautiful garden. It's ruined. How could you do this to me?"

"I'm sorry, Mom," Saina said. "I am." Tears sprang to her eyes again as she filled with anger. Patrick, you are a stupid, stupid donkey, Saina thought.

Her mom took a deep breath and sighed, "Oh, well. What's done is done, and we can't change that. But you'll have to spend your day in the garden trying to fix it up. I don't think Dad would be too thrilled to see it in the state it is now."

Saina had planned to spend her day quietly reading. "OK, Mom. I'll do the best I can," she said resignedly. "Patrick, you wait!" she added silently.

It didn't take too long for Saina to clean up the garden, because Patrick hadn't left many vegetables to clean up. In a couple of hours she had it nearly completed. She raked up the scraps of vegetables that he'd strewn around, and hoed the areas in which he'd left hoofprints.

She was leaning on the hoe when her mother called from the door, "Saina, could you give me a hand in here for a minute?" Saina was happy to have a change of job, and went inside.

"Can you help me lift up the carpet in the living room, please? There's a lot of work to be done to get this house into shape." As she put a hand on Saina's shoulder, her mom said, "Do you know, I never had a pony when I was your age. I had a rocking horse once, though. But it certainly wasn't much of a jumper!"

Saina smiled with relief. She knew her mom wasn't mad at her anymore, and was trying to make her feel better about things. She followed her into the living room.

Mom had cleared out the furniture and the room was bare. The old, frayed carpet looked worn and ratty from years of wear. Saina could just make out a faint pattern on parts of it. The faded curtains hanging from the windows reminded Saina of an old Dracula movie she had seen, and the windows were so dirty she could hardly see through them.

"This will be the first room we attack," her father had said when they'd arrived.

Already, her mother had lifted all the carpet edges and folded them back toward the middle of the room. Together, she and Saina rolled up the whole carpet, and with much struggling and heaving, managed to drag it out through the hallway and onto the porch.

They returned to lift up the strips of coarse, hairy padding, which had lain under the carpet. Saina rolled up one strip and was just about to drag it toward the door, when she saw something caught in the tangled fibers. She burrowed into the material with her fingers and pulled out a gold ring!

"Mom," Saina called out excitedly. "Look what I found!"

The ring must have been in its hiding place for a long time, but it gleamed in her hand like newly polished gold. It was a single gold band with a dark red stone embedded in it. On either side of this stone were two smaller ones of the same color. The beautiful, simple symmetry made Saina realize that this was a very valuable ring.

"I think this is a wedding ring, Saina!" Saina's mother exclaimed. "It's beautiful!" She rubbed it on her sleeve, and the burnished gold circle glistened in her hand. "It must have been here for years. Probably since the carpet was laid!"

"What do you think we should do with it?" Saina asked.

"The first thing we have to do is try to find who owns it, I guess. Find out whose it is, or was." Her mom peered closely at the ring. "Hmmm, I think it is very old."

"How do we find out whose it is?"

"I guess it must have belonged to someone who lived here. I doubt it belonged to Mr. Irvine. He wasn't married. It must have been someone who lived here before him." Saina's mom pondered for a moment. "We should take it to the police station next week and see if the police can trace its owner. I'll put it in my jewelry box for now, and we'll get the rest of this room cleaned up. Maybe there are some more treasures for us to find among this mess!"

They continued with the unpleasant job. The old padding had gathered decades' worth of dirt and dust that had filtered down through the carpet. The dust made Saina sneeze. She looked carefully as they rolled up the padding, but no more precious jewelry appeared. She staggered out the door with the last roll and threw it on the pile with the rest.

"Thank you, Saina," said her mom. "You can take a break."

Saina thankfully accepted. "Can I take another look at the ring, Mom?" she asked. Her mom nodded, and Saina ran through to the bedroom and picked up the ring from where it lay among her mother's jewelry. She slipped the ring onto her finger and held it up in front of her. It sparkled and gleamed in the light. What a find!

Chapter 6

A Friend

Before school on Monday, Saina stopped to talk to one of her new classmates, Aimee Newton. Aimee was a slim, curly haired girl with a friendly manner that Saina found easy to respond to. They had talked briefly last week, and Saina found out that Aimee also recently moved into the area and lived on a farm several miles from school. Saina also learned that Aimee had a pony named Bullet, which she rode every day. Aimee was cheerful and fun, and Saina had immediately liked her.

"Hello," Saina said shyly. She was bursting to tell someone her news.

"Hi, Saina," Aimee said. "What did you do this weekend?"

"I helped Mom pull up some old carpet." Saina couldn't contain herself any longer. "And guess what I found under it? A gold wedding ring!"

"Wow!" said Aimee, obviously impressed. "Whose is it?"

"I don't know," replied Saina. "But we think it could be valuable. We're going to try to find its owner."

"There might be a reward for it," Aimee said excitedly.

"I never thought of that," Saina said.

"Yeah!" exclaimed Aimee. "It might be really valuable, and very important to someone, and they'll be so grateful, they'll give you a big reward – maybe even a trip to Disneyland."

"I don't think so, Aimee," laughed Saina. "But then again, if it were enough money to buy a blanket for my pony..."

"Did you get a pony?" Aimee interrupted excitedly.

"Well... " Saina started to tell her about the donkey, but suddenly couldn't. Someone who had their own pony wouldn't feel any enthusiasm for an old donkey. She felt embarrassed, and blushed. She hesitated and then said, "Well, yes, I did get..."

"You got a pony!" cried Aimee. "When did it arrive? Why didn't you tell me? What does it look like? What have you named it? Can I see it?" Her ponytail bobbed up and down as she got more and more excited.

"She's named Dream. But she's very young, and I don't want any visitors until she's settled in and used to me."

Saina heard the words coming from her own mouth as though someone else were saying them. She felt sick. What was she doing? She hadn't meant to tell a huge lie like that. But she just couldn't tell Aimee that she had a donkey. Aimee would have laughed, and Saina just couldn't bear the thought of being laughed at over Patrick.

Aimee's excitement subsided, "Oh, yes. I understand."

But Saina could see that she really didn't understand. In fact, she looked hurt.

Then Aimee smiled and said, "Saina, I'm so happy for you. I just can't wait till we can go riding together on the weekends. Won't it be great!" She then began racing up and down the hallway, making neighing sounds as though she were a wild horse. Saina laughed at her antics, but inside she felt awful.

What had encouraged her to make up such a story? Could it be undone? Or would she have to keep telling lies?

Chapter 7

Making Progress

Saina burst through the door and called out, "Hey, Mom!"

"I'm in the bathroom with Pete, Saina," her mom answered.

Saina ran through and found her mother bathing one-year-old Pete.

"How was school?" her mother asked.

"Great," said Saina. "I've made a new friend named Aimee. Did you find anything out about the ring?"

"Well, yes. And it's both a good-news and bad-news story, I'm afraid," her mom said as she lifted Pete out of the bathtub and wrapped him in a large towel. "Let me just put Pete's clothes into the laundry hamper and I'll tell you all about it."

She handed Pete to Saina, and walked through to the laundry room by the back door. Saina remembered the clean laundry room in their old house. She thought of the freshly painted cupboards and the beautiful, blue-tiled floor. Here, the laundry room had a bare, concrete floor and two old, concrete tubs. Saina still really missed their nice house in the city.

Saina carried Pete to her parents' bedroom and took the ring out of the jewelry box. It looked even more beautiful than she remembered. The dark red stones seemed to flash with their own rich light, and the gold shone like firelight.

She took the ring into the kitchen and sat down at the table with Pete on her lap. He smiled at her and said, "Saina."

"Good boy, Pete," laughed Saina as she tickled him. He giggled and wiggled away from her tickling fingers. Saina wondered what her mother's news would be. What had she meant by "good news and bad news"? Had she found the owner of the ring?

Saina's mother came in and sat down beside Saina and Pete. "Well," she began, "I called the real-estate agent who we bought the house through, and the good news she told me is that before Mr. Irvine lived here, the house used to belong to a Mr. and Mrs. Taylor. The bad news is she had no idea where they live now, or even if they're still alive. After all, Mr. Irvine owned the place for thirty years. So I looked in the phone book, and there are no Taylors in this area, but there are over eighty in the city. I'm certainly not going to call them all! I also called the police station, and the police are going to check their files and call me back."

Saina's mother paused. "So, in the meantime, you have a very valuable ring in your care. Look after it," she warned. "Now, I've got something to show you. Close your eyes." She took Pete from Saina's arms, and led her into the living room.

"OK. You can open your eyes now."

What a transformation! The living room had the family's furniture arranged in it. On the wall were paintings and family photos from the old house. The dirty, old wooden floor had been scrubbed and polished so that it shone like glass. The room was filled with the smells of furniture polish and window cleaner. The windows were sparkling clean, and her mom had taken down the old Dracula drapes and replaced them with new, colorful curtains. The whole room looked so bright and cheerful compared to the dull, smelly, old living room of only a day ago, that Saina could hardly believe she was in the same room.

"I love it!"

Saina's mother glowed with pride. "I told you we could bring out the character of this place," she said. "All it needs is a bit of hard work and some redecorating. You wait. We'll get your bedroom looking wonderful before you know it!"

Chapter 8

Saina's Lies

The next morning, Aimee was waiting for Saina at the school gates.

"Hi," said Aimee. "Any more news about the ring?"

"Not really," Saina said. "Except that we think it could belong to one of the Taylors who lived in the house years and years ago. We're going to try to find them, but we don't know where they're living now. Do you know any Taylors?"

"Taylor?" said Aimee. "I don't know any at school, but I'll ask around for you."

"Thanks, Aimee. That would be great."

"No reward and no blanket then," said Aimee. "How's your pony? Can I come and see her soon?"

"Yes, soon," Saina said. "She's really beautiful, a lovely chestnut color." The lies rolled off her tongue as though they were real. She found herself almost believing her own words.

Over the next few weeks, Aimee invited Saina to her house for the weekend several times, but Saina knew that if she went, then she would have to invite Aimee to her place in return. So, she'd turned down every invitation, inventing a weak excuse each time. She would have loved to invite Aimee to stay over. But how could she? It was a good thing Aimee's bus took her in the opposite direction from Saina's home. Otherwise, it would have been too difficult to keep up the charade. Saina desperately hoped her dad would see her need for a pony and get her one soon.

They still sat together at school, but Saina could see that Aimee was puzzled by her reluctance to come and stay for the weekend. Every day, Saina walked a memory tightrope: What had she told Aimee about her pony, and what hadn't she? How long could she keep up the deception? Her stomach tightened in a knot every time Aimee started to talk about ponies. She really wished she had never lied in the first place. How would all this end? Would Patrick the donkey ever be exchanged for the pony of her stories?

Each day she cared for the hated Patrick, Saina nearly wept with the frustration he caused her. He bit her. He tried to kick her. Every time she turned her back, he butted her with his head in an effort to try to get more oats from the bucket. Saina showed him the empty bucket, she held it upside down, she even shook it near Patrick's head, but he never believed he wouldn't find a few spare oat grains hiding at the bottom. The only time he showed any affection toward her was when she brushed him. He leaned into Saina as if he were trying to ask her to brush him longer. The only thing she had managed to teach him was to come when she called. And that, Saina knew, was only because she held up the oat bucket as she called his name!

One Saturday, Saina decided to try to ride Patrick. He wasn't very big, but he was strong, and Saina knew that he could handle her weight.

"At least I can get to ride something," she grumbled at him. He looked at her with disinterest.

Saina held out the oat bucket temptingly, and the greedy Patrick followed her into the yard next to the barn. She waited until he was busy eating his oats, and then leaned against him. He didn't budge, but just kept chewing. She leaned over him and took her feet off the ground. No reaction. Carefully, she eased her body onto his back, and just as carefully, sat up. Patrick lifted his head out of the bucket and turned to look at her as if to say, "What is this all about?"

Then he sat down. He didn't lie down; he sat. His hindquarters dropped to the ground, and he sat back on his haunches. Saina, unable to hold onto anything, slid down Patrick's back and landed, with a bump, in the dirt!

Patrick promptly stood up again, stretched out his neck, curled back his lips, and brayed, "Eee-yaw!" as if he were laughing. Then, once more, he buried his head in the bucket.

Saina was furious. She got up and, out of revenge, grabbed his bucket from him. "That's all you get today!" she said, and turned to go.

Boomf! She'd forgotten about Patrick's habit, and she found herself on the grass again after he butted her from behind, searching for the bucket. Saina struggled to her feet, sputtering with rage.

“You… you… you… stupid donkey! I hate you! I don’t care if I never get a pony! I don’t want to have anything more to do with you!” She picked up the bucket, emptied the rest of the oats over the donkey’s head, and hurled the bucket over the fence. It sailed through the air, until it was easily caught by her friend, Aimee.

Saina's face dropped. She stood and stared at Aimee. It was all over. Her lies about the pony were out. Saina felt overwhelmed. What would her friend think of her now? Her face crumbled and she burst into tears.

"I d-didn't w-want you to c-come until I had m-my pony," she sobbed. "I d-didn't m-mean to lie to you. I'm s-sorry. I haven't g-got a p-pony, only this d-dumb old d-donkey!" She covered her face with her hands and shook with grief.

"That's OK, Saina. I don't care," Aimee said. "I'm still your friend. I'm not upset. I know about your pony. I talked to your father, and he told me the whole story. He says that you've done a great job of looking after the donkey, and he's going to try to get you a pony soon. So it will all work out, you'll see!" Saina felt Aimee's hand patting her back. "But you'll have to learn to ride better than that!"

Through her tears, Saina looked over at Aimee and burst out laughing. Her face burned with embarrassment, but she was relieved that it was all over. The lies. The deceit. The fear of Aimee finding out the truth. It was finally over!

"Come on," said Aimee. "I've got something exciting to tell you."

Saina looked up and smiled. "You're so nice, Aimee. I really am sorry. You don't know how good it is to not have to pretend anymore." Saina hugged her friend. "What are you doing here, anyway?"

"I came out here with Casey King and her grandmother," Aimee said excitedly. "Casey lives next to our farm, and do you know what her grandmother's name is?" She continued without waiting for an answer, "Mrs. Taylor!"

Chapter 9

Good News

Saina's eyes widened. "You mean..."

"Yes!" cried Aimee. "She used to live in your house, and she lost her wedding ring the day they put down the living room carpet, forty years ago! It was an old family heirloom, and she is so pleased to get it back. Come on, she's over at your place telling your mom and dad about her old home and all sorts of other things."

Saina carefully shut the gate, and the two girls went over to the house, where Mrs. Taylor was waiting.

"I'm just so grateful to you, Saina," said the old woman as she gave Saina a big hug. She looked about seventy, and she had a kind, wrinkled face. "My husband died two years ago, and having this ring will mean so much to me now. It's like getting an old friend back."

Saina smiled at Aimee and gave her hand a quick squeeze.

Aimee said, "I was telling Casey about the ring and your search for a Mrs. Taylor, and she told me that her grandmother is a Mrs. Taylor, and one thing led to another, and well, here we are!"

Everybody smiled because Aimee looked so pleased with herself.

Then Mrs. Taylor said, "Saina, I've had a good talk with your parents about what I can do to thank you, and I think I have just the thing. Do you know that when I lived here, my daughter had a pony and used to ride it everywhere? Now she lives on a farm not too far from here, and her daughter, Casey's cousin, has gone to live in the city." Her eyes twinkled. "She actually owes me a favor or two. I'm pretty sure that I could get you a saddle and bridle, plus one or two other odds and ends you'll find handy."

Saina's face lit up, and she eagerly looked at her parents.

"They also know lots of people in the pony world," continued Mrs. Taylor. "And I'd be happy to get you a good pony."

A pony! Did Mrs. Taylor say *a pony?* Saina could hardly believe her ears. She barely heard Mrs. Taylor's next words.

"Your parents can pay me back if and when they choose." Mrs. Taylor stopped talking and waved her arm around. "I can see my old home has gotten a bit run-down over the years, and I'm very happy to see a young family living here. Already I can see what you and your parents have done to fix it up. Your mom has invited me to come back any time, and I just might take her up on that offer to see how things are going. Well, what do you think, Saina?"

Saina sat there in stunned delight. She looked at her parents and saw in their faces that they had already accepted Mrs. Taylor's generous offer, and that all she had to do was agree. Not trusting her voice, she nodded vigorously.

Then Mrs. Taylor stood up and said, "Well, come on, Aimee and Casey. We'd better get these things under way, or Saina will think it's all just a dream!"

Chapter 10

The Last Word

Saina spoke quietly to Aimee as everybody walked out to the car. "Thank you for being such a good friend to me, Aimee," she said. "You must come out soon and stay for the weekend. You can have a ride on my donkey," she laughed.

"I can't wait," replied Aimee. "I've never ridden a donkey. It'll be cool!"

Saina and her family waved good-bye as the car pulled out of the driveway. Then they turned to walk back into the house. They all stopped and stared. There, in the garden, eating the last of the cabbage, was Patrick.

"Oh, no!" cried Saina. "I know I closed that gate, Mom!"

They chased Patrick out of the garden and back into the field through the open gate.

"Honestly, Mom. I closed the gate," Saina said earnestly. "I know I did!"

"You must not have done it properly," replied Saina's mom as she secured the bolt. "Really, Saina!"

They began walking back to the house, with Saina still protesting, when suddenly from behind them came a loud "Eee-yaw!" and out trotted Patrick!

"What!" yelled Saina's mom. "I know I closed that gate. Something weird is going on here. I think I owe you an apology, Saina."

They herded Patrick back into the field, closed the gate carefully, and stepped back to watch. They saw Patrick walk up to the gate, push his nose into the frame, and neatly slide back the handle. He then butted the gate with his head, and it swung open!

"Well, I'll be..." said Saina's dad, and everybody burst out laughing.

"Eee-yaw," brayed Patrick, and he headed for the garden.

"Oh, no you don't!" cried Saina as she quickly grabbed him. With her father helping, they managed to pull the reluctant Patrick through the gate and into the big field. Her dad slammed the gate shut and attached a chain. He called out to the donkey, "Get out of this one, Patrick!"

Patrick immediately lowered his head and began cropping the grass, as if eating cabbage was the last thing on his mind.

"It was a good thing Patrick made a mess of the garden and I asked Saina to come and help me roll up the carpet," said Saina's mom as they sat around talking about the events of the day. "Or we may never have even seen the ring."

"And it's a good thing I brought Patrick home," Saina's dad said, "or all this may not have happened at all!" He winked at Saina.

"Do you know who you have to thank for all this, Saina?" asked her mother.

Saina looked puzzled. Then she saw the smile on her mother's face. She hugged both her parents and shot out the door. She ran happily down the path and over to the field where Patrick was quietly grazing. She climbed the gate and walked over to him. He lifted his head and sniffed at her hands to see if she'd brought any oats.

"Patrick, this may be the last time I say this, but thank you. I almost like you. And you're certainly not stupid." Saina put her arms around his neck and hugged him.

Patrick thought he was about to be forcibly moved again and responded in his usual fashion. He bit her.

Saina screamed and fell back in surprise. She lay on the grass in momentary shock. Then she smiled, began to giggle, and burst into laughter.

Patrick found all this excitement too hard to resist. "Eee-yaw! Eee-yaw!" he called. It sounded as if he were laughing.

From the Author

I used to live in an old house on a small farm just outside Invercargill, New Zealand. That's where the setting for *The Trouble with Patrick* came from.

My family used to own a horse that was a bit of a donkey. Each of my four daughters has, at some stage, asked for a pony, so I understand how much Saina wanted a pony. So far, I've managed to find my daughters alternative pets, and have avoided the expense and upkeep of looking after a pony.

I included the ring as a piece of "buried treasure" to give the story some mystery and excitement. Somehow the farm, my girls' desire for a pony, the donkey, and the ring all ended up in one story.

Alan Whitaker

From the Illustrator

I have been drawing and painting for as long as I can remember. I like drawing and painting many things, but I especially like drawing people. In addition to illustrating children's books, I exhibit drawings and paintings in art galleries around Australia, where I live.

I started illustrating children's books a few years ago and I thoroughly enjoy it. I draw and paint just about every day of the year, which makes me very happy.

I really enjoyed illustrating this book because I have always had a secret yearning to live on a farm and have my own pet donkey. I think donkeys are beautiful, and I found *The Trouble with Patrick* a fun, lively story.

Marjorie Scott

WHEN THINGS GO WRONG
The Long Walk Home
The Trouble with Patrick
The Kids from Quiller's Bend
Laughter Is the Best Medicine
Wild Horses
The Sunday Horse

SOMETHING STRANGE
My Father the Mad Professor
A Theft in Time: Timedetectors II
CD and the Giant Cat
Chocolate!
White Elephants and Yellow Jackets
Dream Boat

ANOTHER TIME, ANOTHER PLACE
Cloudcatcher
Flags
The Dinosaur Connection
Myth or Mystery?
Where Did the Maya Go?
The Journal: Dear Future II

CONFIDENCE AND COURAGE
Imagine This, James Robert
Follow That Spy!
Who Will Look Out for Danny?
Fuzz and the Glass Eye
Bald Eagles
Cottle Street

Written by **Alan Whitaker**
Illustrated by **Marjorie Scott**
Edited by **Frances Bacon**
Designed by **Kristie Rogers**

02 01 00
10 9 8 7 6 5 4 3

Distributed in the United States by
Rigby
a division of Reed Elsevier Inc.
P.O. Box 797
Crystal Lake, IL 60039-0797

Printed by Colorcraft, Hong Kong
ISBN: 0-7901-1696-0